Just Be

Written and Illustrated by
Joy A. Hittner

ISBN-13: 978-1470175795
ISBN-10: 1470175797

This morning Delia didn't have anything to do. She didn't feel happy. Mom was busy painting in the family room. When Delia asked her what she should do, Mom never stopped painting. She just shrugged her shoulders and told her that she should just be good, and that would be a big help.

Delia went to find her dad. He was paying bills at his desk. His face had kind of a pinched look, and when Delia asked him what she should do, he just rubbed his hands through his hair and told her that whatever she did, she should just try to be quiet.

When Delia went to look for her brother in his room, he was busy on the phone talking to a friend. Delia started playing with his football, and he gave her an impatient look. So she asked him what she *could* do, but he just rolled his eyes and told her that she should just be gone.

Just then the doorbell rang. Delia ran to see who it could be, and there was Grampa's face peeking in through the window beside the door.

"A little bird told me that you needed someone to spend some time with you," he said with a smile.

"Grampa, birds don't talk," Delia giggled, hugging his face with her warm hands.

"They do when you know how to listen."

"How do you listen?"

"Well, you just have to learn how to . . . be!"

"Be what? Be good?" Delia questioned.

"No."

"Be quiet?"

"Sometimes that helps," Grampa replied.

"Behave?"

"No, . . . just be."

"But, how do I learn how to just be?" Delia questioned.

"Well," Grampa began as he came into the house. He took his coat off and sat down in the big over-stuffed chair that was his favorite. He made a cozy space for Delia to sit beside him. It felt like a little nest just for her.

"Well, you have to practice. You just be . . . in your memory and in your right now time. You just be . . . in all the special places and in remembered spaces. Just be.

Think of a gentle snowy day, your face is turned up to the clouds. Feel the memory of each snowflake as it lands on your cheek soft as a whisper, and in a moment, it melts into a liquid diamond on your skin. Just be.

"Remember filling feeders for winter birds. You scoop out a handful and hold it out. Wait! Wait quiet and still. Breathe soft, until chickadee lands upon your fingers to empty your hand and fill your heart. Just be.

Imagine standing by the horse's stall bedded deep with clean wood shavings full of the scent of pine. The mare's breath blowing, her lips reaching for fresh hay, munching slowly, eyes are closed in half sleep. Inhale the smells, and feel the peace. Just be.

Picture yourself lying in a hammock. Pine branches blowing above. Needles are brushing together playing the music of trees. Birds join in with their song. You sway to the rhythm of a friendly breeze, and sink slowly into a comfortable space between waking and dreaming. Just be.

Recall watching a slate-gray summer sky. Clouds are building and moving overhead; wind worrying grasses and hair and clothes on the line; rumbling heard in the distance. Cooling drops and cooler air find your face. The smell of rain is on the wind; lines of lightning like silvery spider webs across the sky. Just be.

See yourself spreading your blanket on grasses deep and soft beside a brook; the sound of water rushing over rocks; fluttering butterfly and fragrant flower. Sunshine through the branches makes freckles on your face. Your heart slows with the calm of it all. Just be.

Pretend you stop along a deer path to enjoy the colors on a cool fall afternoon. The sound of calling on wings far overhead; V-shaped flocks of geese encouraging one another, and following the path their kind has taken for thousands of years through a sky that is more blue than the crayons in your box. Just be.

Catch a breeze coming far from some unknown place. It stops for a time to dance upon your skin and frolic through your hair. Listen! It carries stories of towns and forests and oceans you can only see in your imagination. Just be.

Look west at the end of the day. The sun so slowly sinks, splashing color across the sky and blackening the horizon below. The land grows quiet and hushed. Time slows, your breath slows, your mind slows . . . ready for darkness . . . soft. Just be.

Put your hand in my hand; fingers laced, intertwined, making pathways for sharing warm, safe feelings; a touching time of together. Breathe, smile, hang on tight, hang on gently. Hang on, even after you let go. Just be . . . in the smile of our touch, in the smile our love. Just . . . be.

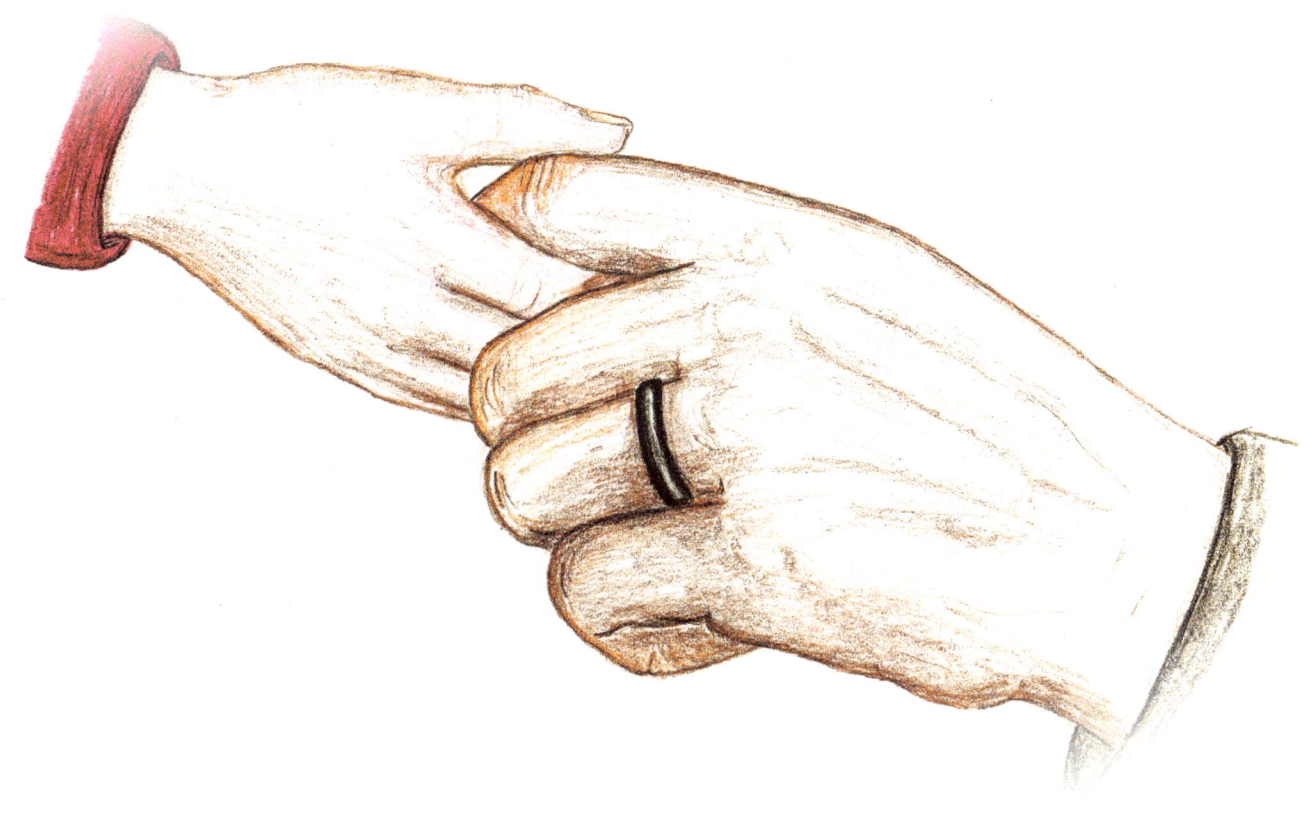

From childhood on, Joy Hittner has always had a love of natural places and quiet spaces. Her desire to share the peace and connection she experiences in these settings has flowed smoothly into her writing. Joy tries to share this sense of connection with all things, often using the medium of "old wisdom" in the form of grandparents to help focus on the feelings children may experience in natural settings.

JoyAHittner.com

Facebook.com/AuthorJoyAHittner

www.ingramcontent.com/pod-product-compliance
Lightning Source LLC
Chambersburg PA
CBHW060807290526
45792CB00005BA/1556